STEVE JAY

The Emberwood Prophecy

Contents

The Mysterious Arrival

The sun dipped below the horizon, casting long shadows over the quaint town of Emberwood. In the fading light, the cobblestone streets were quiet, the air thick with anticipation. At the heart of the town stood an ancient oak tree, its gnarled branches reaching out like skeletal fingers against the deepening twilight.

Amidst this eerie atmosphere, a figure emerged from the shadows. Cloaked in tattered fabric that seemed to absorb what little light remained, the stranger moved with a purposeful yet haunting grace. Their eyes, glinting like shards of obsidian, surveyed the town with an unsettling intensity.

At the edge of the square, young Elara stood, her eyes wide with curiosity and a hint of fear. She was a girl of uncommon intelligence, her inquisitive nature often leading her into trouble. Tonight was no exception. She watched the stranger approach, her senses tingling with a mixture of excitement and dread.

The stranger's voice, when it came, sent shivers down Elara's spine. "Beware, child," they rasped, the words hanging in the air like a dark omen. "The Emberwood Prophecy awakens. The ancient powers stir, and the town is not as safe as it seems."

Elara's heart pounded in her chest. "What do you mean?" she stammered, her voice barely audible above the rustling leaves. But the stranger had already turned away, disappearing into the night as mysteriously as they had come.

With a sense of foreboding, Elara hurried home, her mind racing with questions. Who was the stranger, and what did they know about the prophecy? The legends whispered of a time when the town would face a great trial, but most dismissed it as mere folklore.

Inside her small, candlelit room, Elara opened an ancient tome passed down through generations. Its pages were yellowed and fragile, filled with cryptic symbols and faded ink. As she deciphered the text, the words seemed to come alive, painting a vivid picture of a world long forgotten.

The prophecy spoke of a chosen one, a guardian who would rise to challenge the darkness. Elara's eyes widened in realization. Could it be her? The weight of destiny settled on her shoulders, and she knew there was no turning back.

Outside, the wind howled like a mournful spirit, carrying with it the echoes of a forgotten time. Emberwood, once a haven of peace, was on the brink of an unimaginable journey. And Elara, with her newfound knowledge, was thrust into the heart of the storm, where the line between myth and reality blurred, and the true test of her courage was yet to come.

Unveiling the Prophecy

Morning dawned, casting a golden hue over the tranquil town of Emberwood. Despite the serene facade, an undercurrent of tension gripped the townsfolk. Elara, burdened by the stranger's cryptic message, found herself drawn back to the ancient oak tree where she had encountered the enigmatic figure the night before.

Beneath the sprawling branches, she met with the town historian, a wise old woman named Agatha, whose eyes twinkled with ancient wisdom. Agatha had always been Elara's source of knowledge, her stories weaving a tapestry of Emberwood's past. Today, however, there was a darkness in her gaze.

"The time has come, child," Agatha said, her voice low and grave. "The Emberwood Prophecy is no mere tale. It is a legacy passed down through generations, a warning etched in the very soul of this town."

As Agatha spoke, she led Elara to a hidden chamber beneath the town square. The walls were adorned with intricate murals, depicting a hero facing unimaginable trials, the weight of the world upon their shoulders. Among the images, one stood out—a blazing ember encased in an ancient sigil.

"This is the symbol of the prophecy," Agatha explained, her fingers tracing the lines of the emblem. "The ember represents hope amidst the darkness, a flicker of light that can vanquish even the deepest shadows. But it requires a guardian, someone brave enough to face the looming threat."

Elara's pulse quickened. She realized the magnitude of her role as the chosen one. The responsibility weighed heavily on her young shoulders, but determination sparked in her eyes.

Together, they pored over scrolls and texts, deciphering the ancient language of the prophecy. The words spoke of a celestial alignment, a rare event that would awaken the dormant powers within Emberwood. A chill settled in Elara's bones as she realized the alignment was imminent.

As night fell once more, Elara and Agatha ventured into the forest surrounding Emberwood, guided by the prophecy's clues. Their path was lit by the ethereal glow of fireflies, leading them to a hidden grove where ancient stones, etched with long-forgotten runes, stood in a circle.

With bated breath, they waited. The air crackled with energy, and the stars above shimmered in an otherworldly dance. Suddenly, a tremor ran through the earth, and the stones began to resonate with a deep, melodic hum.

Elara's heart raced as she felt the power of the prophecy coursing through her veins. The grove seemed to come alive, whispers of ancient voices filling the air. The prophecy was awakening, and Emberwood's fate hung in the balance.

In the midst of the suspense, Elara understood that her journey had only just begun. The challenges ahead were daunting, but she was no longer alone. With Agatha's guidance and the ancient prophecy as her beacon, she steeled herself for the trials to come, ready to face the darkness and protect the town she loved.

Dark Secrets

Emberwood's once-tranquil facade began to crack, revealing hidden fissures beneath the surface. Whispers of the awakening prophecy spread like wildfire, stirring both fear and fascination among the townsfolk. Elara, now aware of her role as the guardian, felt the weight of their expectations pressing down on her shoulders.

Amidst the mounting tension, Elara delved deeper into Emberwood's history, seeking answers to the enigmatic prophecy. She spent countless hours in the town's archives, poring over ancient scrolls and texts. One night, as the moon hung low in the sky, she uncovered a long-lost journal belonging to a scholar named Elysia.

Elysia's entries spoke of an artifact—the Emberstone—a powerful relic rumored to be the key to mastering the prophecy's magic. The journal described a hidden chamber deep within the Emberwood Forest where the Emberstone was said to be hidden. With newfound determination, Elara resolved to find it before the forces of darkness could lay their hands on it.

Armed with Elysia's journal and a flickering lantern, Elara ventured into the heart of the forest. The trees loomed like silent sentinels, their twisted branches casting eerie shadows on the forest floor. Every rustle of leaves, every distant howl of a night creature, sent chills down her spine.

After what felt like an eternity, Elara stumbled upon the hidden chamber. Its entrance, concealed behind a curtain of ivy, opened into a vast, underground cavern. The air inside was thick with ancient magic, and the chamber was adorned with intricate runes glowing softly in the darkness.

In the center of the chamber stood a pedestal, upon which rested the Emberstone—a jewel of mesmerizing brilliance, pulsating with an inner fire. Elara's breath caught in her throat as she approached, her hand trembling as she reached out to touch the artifact.

But just as her fingers brushed the Emberstone's surface, the chamber trembled, and the runes on the walls began to glow with an ominous intensity. Elara realized she was not alone. Dark figures emerged from the shadows, their eyes glinting with malevolence.

They were the Cult of Shadows, a secretive group that had long sought the power of the Emberstone for their nefarious purposes. Elara's heart pounded as she faced them, her determination flickering like a candle in a gust of wind.

A fierce battle ensued, the clash of magic and steel echoing through the chamber. Elara fought with a newfound strength, channeling the power of the prophecy to fend off her adversaries. The chamber trembled with the intensity of their struggle, the very earth seeming to rebel against the dark forces that sought to corrupt its magic.

Amidst the chaos, Elara managed to seize the Emberstone, its fiery glow resonating with her own inner power. With a burst of energy, she unleashed a blinding light that engulfed the Cult of Shadows, banishing them from the chamber.

Breathing heavily, Elara clutched the Emberstone to her chest, realizing the magnitude of her achievement. The artifact, now in her possession, represented both hope and danger—a beacon of light in the encroaching darkness, yet a magnet for those who sought to extinguish it.

As she made her way back to Emberwood, Elara knew that the battle was far from over. The Cult of Shadows had been thwarted, but they were merely a harbinger of the challenges to come. With the Emberstone as her ally, she steeled herself for the trials ahead, determined to protect her town and fulfill the prophecy's ancient promise.

The Enigmatic Symbols

In the aftermath of her harrowing encounter with the Cult of Shadows, Elara found herself haunted by the memory of their malevolent eyes. With the Emberstone clutched tightly in her hand, she retreated to the safety of her room, seeking solace in the glow of a single candle.

As the flickering flame cast dancing shadows on the walls, Elara carefully examined the Emberstone. Its surface was adorned with intricate symbols, ancient runes that seemed to pulse with a life of their own. Determined to understand the artifact's power, she delved into her studies, hoping to decipher the enigmatic symbols that adorned the Emberstone.

Night after night, Elara poured over dusty tomes and scrolls, her mind a whirlwind of theories and speculations. Hours turned into days, and days into weeks, but her efforts finally bore fruit. One night, as the moon hung low in the sky, she made a breakthrough.

The symbols on the Emberstone, she realized, were part of an ancient language—a language of magic and power that had been all but forgotten. With trembling hands, she translated the inscriptions, unlocking the secrets of the artifact. The Emberstone, it seemed, was a conduit—a channel through which the prophecy's magic could be harnessed.

Armed with this newfound knowledge, Elara set out to explore the depths of Emberwood, guided by the Emberstone's faint, inner glow. The artifact seemed to pulse with anticipation, leading her to a series of hidden chambers scattered throughout the town.

In these chambers, she discovered relics of the past—ancient artifacts imbued with the same mysterious power as the Emberstone. Each discovery added a piece to the puzzle, revealing the extent of the prophecy's influence on Emberwood. It was a legacy that stretched back centuries, a tapestry woven with threads of magic and destiny.

But even as Elara uncovered the town's hidden secrets, a sense of unease settled over Emberwood. Strange occurrences became commonplace— a shadowy figure glimpsed in the corner of the eye, a whisper of voices carried on the wind. The town's once-vibrant atmosphere was replaced by an oppressive silence, broken only by the cawing of distant crows.

One fateful night, as Elara delved deeper into her research, she stumbled upon a chilling revelation. The symbols on the Emberstone were not just a language; they were a key—a key that could unlock a portal to a realm of unimaginable power. It was a power that the Cult of Shadows sought to control, a power that could tip the balance between light and darkness.

With a sinking feeling, Elara realized that the prophecy was far more complex than she had ever imagined. The fate of Emberwood hung in the balance, and she was its last hope. As she gazed at the Emberstone, its fiery glow seemed to flicker with urgency, as if urging her to embrace her destiny.

In the heart of the night, under the weight of her newfound knowledge, Elara made a solemn vow. She would protect Emberwood at any cost, even if it meant facing the darkest corners of the prophecy. With determination burning in her eyes, she set out to confront the shadows that lurked on the town's outskirts, ready to face whatever challenges lay ahead.

A Race Against Time

The night air in Emberwood crackled with tension as Elara stepped out of her home, the Emberstone cradled in her hands. Her heart raced with a mixture of fear and determination. The cryptic symbols on the artifact glowed softly, reflecting the pale light of the moon. Every fiber of her being resonated with the power of the prophecy, urging her to act.

With each passing day, the celestial alignment drew nearer, the stars shifting into a pattern that had not been seen in centuries. Elara knew that when the alignment occurred, the prophecy's magic would reach its peak, and the forces of darkness would be at their strongest. Time was running out, and she could not afford to wait.

Guided by the Emberstone's gentle glow, Elara ventured into the heart of Emberwood Forest. The ancient trees loomed like silent sentinels, their twisted branches casting eerie shadows on the forest floor. The air was thick with the scent of damp earth and moss, and the distant hoot of an owl added to the ominous ambiance.

As she walked deeper into the forest, Elara sensed a presence, a malevolent force that seemed to coil around the trees like a predatory serpent. The Cult of Shadows, she realized, was close. Their whispers of dark magic slithered through the air, and Elara tightened her grip on the Emberstone, ready for whatever lay ahead.

In a clearing bathed in moonlight, she confronted the cultists—a group of cloaked figures with eyes that gleamed like shards of obsidian. Their leader, a sinister figure with a twisted staff, sneered at her. "So, the chosen one has come to play," he hissed, his voice echoing with malice.

The battle that ensued was fierce and unrelenting. Elara's every movement was fueled by the power of the prophecy, her magic clashing with the dark forces that sought to engulf Emberwood. Spells flew through the air like deadly fireworks, illuminating the night with bursts of vivid colors.

The cultists fought with a desperation born of fanaticism, their eyes ablaze with a fervent belief in their dark cause. Elara, however, fought with a different kind of conviction—a deep-rooted love for her town and a determination to protect its people.

With a surge of power, Elara channeled the Emberstone's energy, unleashing a blinding wave of light that enveloped the cultists. Their screams echoed through the forest as they were banished, their forms dissipating like smoke in the wind.

But the victory was short-lived. The cult's leader, though weakened, remained standing, his eyes filled with a fanatical zeal. He raised his staff, calling upon forbidden incantations that tore at the fabric of reality.

Elara, her strength waning, summoned the last reserves of her magic. With a whispered incantation, she unleashed a torrent of flames that engulfed the cultist. His screams pierced the night as he was consumed by the inferno, leaving nothing but ashes in his wake.

As the echoes of battle faded, Elara sank to her knees, the Emberstone clattering to the forest floor. She had prevailed, but the cost had been high.

The forest, once a sanctuary, now felt like a realm of shadows and sorrow.

With a heavy heart, Elara picked up the Emberstone, its glow flickering weakly. The celestial alignment loomed closer, and she knew that the final confrontation with the dark forces was imminent. As she stood among the charred remains of the cultists, a steely resolve settled over her.

The fate of Emberwood hung in the balance, and Elara was determined to face the impending darkness head-on. With the Emberstone in hand, she set her sights on the town, her steps resolute and her spirit unyielding. The race against time had begun, and she would not rest until the prophecy's magic was harnessed, and Emberwood was saved from the looming catastrophe.

Betrayal in the Shadows

Emberwood, once vibrant, now lay shrouded in a heavy blanket of anticipation. Elara, having repelled the cultists in the forest, returned home with the Emberstone, her heart heavy with the weight of her responsibilities. She sought solace in the company of her closest friend, Aiden, a kindred spirit who had stood by her side since childhood.

As the two friends sat in the dim glow of Elara's chamber, their conversation was laced with a sense of foreboding. Aiden's eyes, once filled with playful mischief, were clouded with worry. "Elara," he said, his voice barely above a whisper, "I fear that not all in Emberwood are as loyal as they seem."

Elara furrowed her brow, her intuition tingling with unease. "What do you mean, Aiden?"

He hesitated, his gaze shifting away for a moment before locking onto hers. "I overheard whispers in the market today—rumors that there are those among us who sympathize with the Cult of Shadows. They believe that harnessing the prophecy's power could bring about a new order, even if it means embracing the darkness."

Dread settled in the pit of Elara's stomach. She had suspected that the cult's influence ran deeper than she had initially thought, but the idea that some of her own townsfolk might be conspiring with them sent chills down her spine.

Aiden's voice trembled with urgency. "We must be cautious, Elara. Trust no one completely, not until we can unveil the true extent of this betrayal."

Night fell over Emberwood, and a bone-chilling mist cloaked the town. Elara, her mind racing with thoughts of betrayal and loyalty, decided to investigate further. Guided by Aiden's warning, she slipped out into the darkness, the Emberstone clutched tightly in her hand.

In the shadows, she overheard hushed conversations and exchanged glances laden with hidden meaning. A feeling of paranoia settled over her as she navigated the web of deceit, her senses alert to every movement and sound.

As she approached the outskirts of town, she saw a flicker of movement in the distance. Silhouetted against the moonlit sky, a figure darted into the trees, and Elara followed, her footsteps soundless on the damp forest floor.

She found herself in a hidden glade, where a group of townsfolk, faces masked by shadows, gathered around a dark altar. In the center of the altar lay an ancient tome, its pages adorned with symbols identical to those on the Emberstone. Elara's heart clenched with realization—this was a secret meeting of the cult sympathizers, performing a forbidden ritual.

Among the gathered, she recognized familiar faces—people she had once called friends, now shrouded in betrayal. Aiden stood among them, his eyes distant, his loyalty seemingly shattered.

With a shock, Elara realized the extent of the deception. Aiden, her closest confidant, had been swayed by the cult's promises of power and a new world order. Betrayal cut through her like a blade, leaving wounds deeper than any physical injury.

In a voice laced with anger and sorrow, Elara confronted him, demanding answers. Aiden's eyes flickered with a mix of guilt and defiance, revealing the internal struggle he faced. He spoke of disillusionment, of a desire for something more than the mundane existence Emberwood offered.

But Elara, her determination unyielding, refused to let his reasons justify his betrayal. With the Emberstone blazing in her hand, she channeled the prophecy's power, forming a barrier that held the cult sympathizers captive, preventing their dark ritual from reaching its fruition.

As the ritual's power surged against her shield, Elara's resolve hardened. With a surge of energy, she banished the cultists, including Aiden, from the glade, their cries of anger and frustration fading into the night.

With Aiden's betrayal weighing heavily on her heart, Elara knew that the road ahead would be treacherous. The bond of trust between her and the townsfolk had been shattered, leaving her isolated in the fight against the Cult of Shadows.

As she clutched the Emberstone, its warmth a reminder of her purpose, Elara steeled herself for the battles yet to come. The shadows in Emberwood had grown darker, but she refused to succumb to despair. The prophecy's power surged within her, a beacon of hope amid the betrayal, guiding her toward the final confrontation that loomed on the horizon.

The Forbidden Ritual

The night hung heavy over Emberwood, a shroud of darkness that seemed to swallow the very stars in the sky. Elara, her heart heavy with the recent betrayal of her closest friend, stood at the edge of the forest, the Emberstone pulsating with a fierce, determined light in her hands. The town, once a sanctuary of peace, now felt like a battleground, the air thick with tension and fear.

The whispers of the Cult of Shadows lingered on the wind, carrying with them a chilling promise of impending doom. Elara knew that their plan was reaching its climax. The celestial alignment, the key to the prophecy's full power, was mere days away. It was during this rare cosmic event that the cult intended to perform the forbidden ritual, harnessing the prophecy's magic to plunge Emberwood into eternal darkness.

With a sense of urgency burning in her chest, Elara set out to gather allies. She knew that she couldn't face the cult alone, not now. As she traversed the quiet streets of Emberwood, her eyes fell upon faces she had known all her life. Suspicion and fear marked the townsfolk's expressions, a stark contrast to the camaraderie that had once bound them together.

Her first stop was the house of Rowan, the town's skilled blacksmith and a seasoned warrior. She found him in his workshop, the clanging of metal against metal filling the air. His broad shoulders were tense, his eyes weary but sharp.

"Rowan," Elara began, her voice steady despite the turmoil within her. "We need your strength. The cult is planning a ritual during the celestial alignment. We must stop them."

Rowan's gaze met hers, and a flicker of recognition and determination sparkled in his eyes. "I've heard whispers of their plans," he admitted. "I'll stand with you, Elara. Together, we'll defend Emberwood."

Emboldened by Rowan's support, Elara sought out Sylas, the town's wise herbalist and healer. She found him in his herb-filled sanctuary, his hands gently caressing the leaves of ancient plants.

"Sylas," she implored, her voice carrying the weight of the town's hopes. "We need your knowledge. The cult is performing a ritual, and we must find a way to counter their dark magic."

Sylas, his eyes kind and knowing, nodded solemnly. "I've been studying ancient texts, searching for a way to disrupt their magic. There's an old incantation, a forgotten spell that might work. But it requires a rare ingredient—a moonbloom, found only in the heart of the Moonlit Grove."

Elara's resolve hardened. She would venture into the Moonlit Grove, a place rumored to be haunted by ancient spirits, to secure the moonbloom. With the support of Rowan, whose blacksmithing skills could fashion a protective amulet, she prepared for the perilous journey.

Under the silvery glow of the moon, Elara, Rowan, and Sylas set out toward the Moonlit Grove. The forest came alive with nocturnal creatures, their eyes glinting in the darkness. The air was heavy with the scent of blooming flowers and the eerie silence of the night.

As they entered the grove, the atmosphere changed. The moon's rays filtered through the thick canopy, casting a spectral light on the ancient trees. Faint whispers drifted through the air, the voices of long-forgotten spirits that seemed to echo with both sadness and warning.

Guided by Sylas' knowledge, they ventured deeper into the grove. The moonbloom, a delicate flower said to bloom only under the light of a full moon, was their only hope. The trio moved with caution, their senses alert to every rustle and every distant sound.

After what felt like hours, they found it—a cluster of moonblooms, their petals glowing with a soft, ethereal radiance. Elara carefully plucked the rare flowers, her fingers tingling with their magic. The moonlit grove seemed to hold its breath as they retreated, the spirits' whispers growing fainter as they left the haunted sanctuary behind.

Back in Emberwood, Rowan set to work, fashioning the moonbloom into a protective amulet while Sylas prepared the ancient incantation. Elara, her eyes fixed on the celestial tapestry above, felt a mixture of hope and trepidation. The celestial alignment was drawing nearer, its cosmic dance signaling the convergence of the prophecy's power.

As the appointed night fell, the townsfolk gathered in the town square, their eyes filled with both fear and determination. Elara, donning the moonbloom amulet, held the Emberstone high, its fiery glow illuminating her determined face. Rowan and Sylas stood by her side, their presence a reassuring anchor in the storm.

The cultists, led by a new, sinister figure, emerged from the shadows. Their leader, a woman with eyes as cold as ice, sneered at Elara. "You cannot stop us, chosen one," she spat, her voice dripping with disdain. "The ritual will proceed, and Emberwood will bow before the might of the prophecy."

Elara, her grip on the Emberstone unwavering, met the cultist's gaze with steely resolve. "You underestimate the power of unity," she declared, her voice ringing with conviction. "Emberwood's strength lies not in darkness, but in the courage of its people."

With those words, the ritual began. The cultists chanted in a language long forgotten, their voices rising in an unholy harmony. The air crackled with dark energy, the very essence of the prophecy's magic at play.

Elara, her heart pounding, unleashed the ancient incantation Sylas had taught her. The words flowed from her lips like a prayer, weaving a barrier of protective light around the townsfolk. Rowan's blacksmithing skills came to life as he forged a shield, channeling his craftsmanship into a tangible defense against the dark forces.

The air trembled with the clash of magic as the opposing energies met. Elara's amulet glowed brilliantly, its protective aura holding strong against the cultists' dark incantations. The townsfolk, their faces a mix of fear and determination, stood their ground, their collective will a formidable shield against the cult's onslaught.

The battle raged on, the very fabric of reality warping and bending under the strain of the conflicting forces. Elara, her eyes ablaze with the Emberstone's power, stood at the heart of the storm, her every breath a testament to her unwavering determination.

With a final surge of energy, Elara channeled the Emberstone's magic. The artifact blazed with an intensity that outshone the stars themselves, its fiery light engulfing the cultists in a blinding wave of power. Their cries of despair echoed through the night as they were consumed by the brilliance of the prophecy's magic.

The cult's leader, her arrogance shattered, tried to flee, but Elara, fueled by her love for Emberwood and her newfound mastery of the prophecy, pursued her. In a climactic duel, Elara unleashed the full force of the Emberstone, casting the cultist into a vortex of shimmering light. With a scream that reverberated through the night, the

cultist vanished, leaving behind only a lingering echo of her malice.

Emberwood fell silent. The cultists were defeated, their dark ambitions vanquished by the strength of unity and the power of the prophecy. The townsfolk, their faces etched with relief and awe, looked to Elara with newfound reverence. She, the chosen one, had saved them all.

In the aftermath of the battle, as the first light of dawn kissed the horizon, the townsfolk gathered around Elara, their gratitude and admiration shining in their eyes. The once-divided town was now united, their shared struggle against the cult forging bonds that would endure for generations.

Emberwood, bathed in the warm embrace of the morning sun, stood as a testament to the resilience of the human spirit. The shadows of the cult were banished, replaced by the light of hope and the promise of a better tomorrow.

As Elara lowered the Emberstone, its glow fading to a gentle flicker, she knew that her journey was far from over. The prophecy, once a burden, had become a beacon of hope, guiding her toward a future where unity and courage would always triumph over darkness.

With a newfound sense of purpose, Elara looked toward the horizon, her eyes reflecting the dawn of a new era. Emberwood, once on the brink of destruction, was now reborn, its spirit unbreakable, its people stronger than ever before.

And in the heart of the town, beneath the ancient oak tree, a small plaque was placed—a tribute to the bravery of the chosen one and the resilience of

Emberwood. The words inscribed on it echoed through the ages, a reminder of the town's darkest hour and the triumphant light that had emerged from the shadows.

The prophecy had been fulfilled, not in the way the townsfolk had feared, but in a way that surpassed their wildest dreams. Elara, with her courage and determination, had rewritten the fate of Emberwood, proving that even in the face of the most insurmountable challenges, the human spirit would always prevail. And so, as the day unfolded and the townsfolk began to rebuild their lives, they did so with a newfound sense of unity, their shared triumph becoming a legacy that would be passed down through the generations.

Emberwood, once a town on the brink of darkness, had emerged stronger and more resilient than ever before. The prophecy, once a source of fear, was now a testament to the indomitable spirit of its people. And in the hearts of those who had witnessed the town's transformation, a profound belief took root—that no matter how dire the circumstances, as long as there was hope, as long as there were individuals willing to stand against the shadows, the light would always prevail.

Echoes of the Past

Emberwood basked in the warm glow of a new dawn, its people rebuilding their lives amidst the remnants of the past. The town square, once marred by the cult's dark presence, now teemed with life. Laughter and the sounds of construction filled the air as the townsfolk worked together, their shared triumph over the cult fostering a sense of camaraderie that was stronger than ever.

Elara, the town's savior, had become a beacon of hope, her presence inspiring those around her. Yet, beneath her newfound confidence, a shadow of uncertainty lingered. The events of the past weeks had reshaped her, leaving her with questions that danced on the edges of her consciousness.

One quiet evening, as the sun dipped below the horizon, Elara found herself drawn to the town's library—a place she had always sought solace in. The shelves were lined with ancient tomes and scrolls, their pages whispering secrets of times long past. Elara's fingers trailed over the spines, her mind craving knowledge that might provide answers to the lingering mysteries of the prophecy.

Her search led her to a weathered leather-bound book tucked away in a secluded corner. Its pages were filled with illustrations of celestial alignments and cryptic symbols. It spoke of the prophecy's origins, tracing its roots back to an ancient civilization that had once thrived in the very lands Emberwood now stood upon.

Intrigued, Elara delved deeper into the text, her eyes widening with realization. The prophecy was not unique to Emberwood—it was part of a tapestry woven across time and space, a universal truth that transcended the boundaries of individual towns and nations.

As she read, Elara uncovered a chilling revelation. The cult that had threatened Emberwood was just one faction among many, scattered across the world like dark tendrils seeking to exploit the prophecy's power for their own gain. The alignment of the stars, the convergence of cosmic forces—it was all part of a cycle, a recurring event that marked the awakening of the prophecy's magic.

Emberwood, it seemed, was not the first town to face the cult's menace, nor would it be the last. The realization weighed heavily on Elara. The responsibility that had once felt like a burden now seemed like an unending duty, a never-ending battle against the forces of darkness.

Determined to unravel the mysteries of the prophecy, Elara sought the wisdom of Agatha, the town historian. With her keen insight and vast knowledge, Agatha had always been a guiding light in times of uncertainty.

In Agatha's cozy cottage, surrounded by the scent of herbs and ancient scrolls, Elara shared her discoveries. Agatha listened, her eyes narrowing with concern. "The prophecy's magic is a double-edged sword, my dear," she said, her voice laden with wisdom. "It grants great power, but it also attracts those who would misuse it for their own nefarious purposes."

Elara nodded, her mind racing with the implications of Agatha's words. "But how can we protect Emberwood, and other towns like ours, from falling victim to these dark forces?" she asked, her voice laced with determination.

Agatha's gaze softened. "Knowledge is our greatest weapon," she replied. "We must understand the prophecy in its entirety, not just its magic but its history, its purpose. Only then can we hope to thwart the cult and safeguard our world from their machinations."

With Agatha's guidance, Elara delved deeper into her studies. Days turned into weeks, and weeks into months as she immersed herself in ancient texts and forgotten lore. The library became her sanctuary, its hallowed halls witness to her tireless pursuit of knowledge.

One night, as the stars shimmered in the midnight sky, Elara made a breakthrough. She stumbled upon a passage that spoke of a legendary artifact—the Astral Crown—an ancient relic said to hold the power to control the prophecy's magic. The crown was said to be hidden in a long-lost temple, a place of trials and tribulations that would test the very essence of those who sought it.

With newfound determination, Elara set out on a perilous quest to find the Astral Crown. Guided by the cryptic clues in the ancient texts, she journeyed across treacherous terrain, braving dense forests and rugged mountains. Her every step was marked by the weight of the prophecy and the hope that the crown could be the key to ending the cult's menace once and for all.

The journey was arduous, filled with challenges that pushed Elara to her limits. Yet, with each trial she faced, her resolve strengthened. She met allies along the way—brave souls who had also felt the pull of destiny, drawn to the path of protecting their homes from the cult's shadows.

Together, they navigated the labyrinthine depths of the temple, its walls adorned with celestial motifs and enigmatic symbols. The air was thick with an ancient energy, a tangible reminder of the temple's ageless existence. As they delved deeper, the trials grew more perilous, testing not just their physical prowess but also their wits and determination.

In the heart of the temple, they found it—the Astral Crown, resting atop a pedestal adorned with glowing runes. Elara's heart raced as she approached, her fingers trembling as she touched the cool metal of the artifact. Its power surged through her, a potent reminder of the responsibility that now rested upon her shoulders.

But even as she held the

crown, a chilling presence filled the air. The cult, ever watchful, had caught wind of their quest. They descended upon the temple like a swarm of vengeful spirits, their eyes ablaze with malevolence.

A fierce battle ensued, the clash of swords and magic reverberating through the temple's ancient halls. Elara, her grip firm on the Astral Crown, fought with a newfound strength, channeling the artifact's power to fend off the cultists. Her allies, too, fought valiantly, their determination matching her own.

The battle reached its climax in the temple's central chamber, where the cult's leader, a figure shrouded in darkness, confronted Elara. Their eyes locked in a silent exchange of defiance and hatred. The cultist unleashed a torrent of dark magic, their spells crashing against Elara's protective barrier.

With a cry of determination, Elara channeled the Astral Crown's power. The artifact blazed with an otherworldly brilliance, a radiant aura that engulfed the cultist. Their screams echoed through the chamber as they were consumed by the crown's energy, leaving behind only a smoky residue.

The remaining cultists, their leader defeated, fled the temple, their dark ambitions thwarted once more. Elara, her chest heaving with exhaustion, looked at the Astral Crown in her hands. Its power was vast, its potential limitless, but she knew that its true purpose was to protect, not to conquer.

With the crown as her ally, Elara returned to Emberwood, her heart heavy with the knowledge of the challenges that lay ahead. The cult was defeated, but its remnants lingered like a lingering fog, threatening to resurface at any moment.

As she entered the town, the townsfolk greeted her with a mixture of relief and gratitude. The Astral Crown, its glow soft but reassuring, became a symbol of hope, a beacon that lit the way toward a future where the shadows of the cult were but a distant memory.

But even in the midst of their victory, Elara knew that the echoes of the past would never truly fade. The prophecy, with its ancient magic and timeless power, would continue to shape the destinies of those it touched. The cult may have been defeated, but the struggle against the darkness was far from over.

Emberwood, with its resilient people and their indomitable spirit, stood ready to face whatever challenges lay ahead. With the Astral Crown as their guardian, they would forge a future where unity and courage would always triumph over the shadows, a future where the echoes of the past served as a reminder of their strength and determination.

And so, as the night fell and the stars twinkled overhead, Elara stood at the heart of Emberwood, her eyes fixed on the horizon. The Astral Crown rested upon her brow, its power flowing through her like a river of light. The town, once threatened by the cult's darkness, now stood as a testament to the triumph of hope and the resilience of the human spirit.

With a deep breath, Elara faced the future, her heart filled with both trepidation and excitement. The journey was far from over, but she was no longer alone. The people of Emberwood stood beside her, their collective strength a force to be reckoned with.

As she looked at the town she had sworn to protect, Elara knew that the echoes of the past would continue to shape their destinies. But they would face the future together, united by a common purpose and bound by the unbreakable thread of their shared triumph over the cult's darkness.

With a final glance at the stars, Elara turned her gaze back to Emberwood. The night was alive with possibilities, and she was ready to face whatever challenges the future held. The town's story, once marred by the shadows of the cult, was now a tale of resilience, courage, and the enduring power of hope.

And so, beneath the vast expanse of the night sky, Elara and the people of Emberwood embraced the future, their hearts alight with the promise of a new beginning. The echoes of the past faded into the background, replaced by the triumphant melody of a town reborn, its spirit unyielding, its future boundless.

Whispers of the Shadows

Time passed in Emberwood, the town gradually healing from the wounds inflicted by the cult. The Astral Crown, its power harnessed by Elara, stood as a silent guardian, casting a protective aura over the town. The streets were bustling with life once more, and the scars of the past seemed to fade into the background.

Yet, in the quiet moments between dusk and dawn, whispers of the shadows still lingered. The townsfolk, though resilient, found themselves haunted by the memory of the cult's darkness. Elara, too, felt the weight of their fears pressing down on her shoulders.

One night, as the moon hung low in the sky, Elara stood at the edge of Emberwood, her eyes fixed on the dense forest beyond. The forest, once a sanctuary, now seemed to hold secrets that sent shivers down her spine. She sensed a lingering malevolence, a presence that refused to fade away.

With a heavy heart, Elara decided to venture into the forest, guided by an instinct that whispered of an impending threat. The Astral Crown, warm against her skin, bolstered her courage as she stepped into the shadows.

The forest was silent, save for the rustle of leaves and the distant hoot of an owl. Elara's senses were on high alert, her every step cautious as she moved deeper into the heart of the trees. The air grew thick with an unnatural chill, sending a shiver down her spine.

As she ventured further, Elara stumbled upon a clearing bathed in an eerie blue light. At its center stood a strange, ancient obelisk, its surface adorned with cryptic runes. The obelisk pulsed with a dark energy, sending ripples through the air.

Elara approached the obelisk, her eyes narrowing with suspicion. It was unlike anything she had ever seen, and its presence seemed to resonate with the same malevolence she had felt in the forest. With a deep breath, she reached out to touch its surface.

The moment her fingers made contact, a surge of images flooded her mind—a vision of a long-forgotten prophecy, one that spoke of a cosmic event known as the Shadow Eclipse. The eclipse, a phenomenon that occurred once in a millennia, was said to awaken ancient beings from the depths of the shadows, beings hungry for the power of the Astral Crown.

Dread settled in the pit of Elara's stomach. The vision revealed a truth that sent chills down her spine—the cult's remnants, desperate and vengeful, sought to exploit the upcoming Shadow Eclipse to unleash darkness upon Emberwood once more.

With newfound determination, Elara raced back to town, her heart pounding with urgency. The Astral Crown, though powerful, was not invincible, and she knew that the cult's dark ambitions could not be taken lightly. She needed allies, trusted friends who had proven their mettle in the face of adversity.

Her first stop was Rowan's forge. She found him amidst a shower of sparks, his muscular arms working the anvil with practiced skill. "Rowan," she called out, her voice urgent. "We have a new threat. The cult's remnants plan to strike during the upcoming Shadow Eclipse. We must prepare."

Rowan wiped sweat from his brow, his eyes narrowing with concern. "I'll gather the town's militia," he declared, his voice firm. "We won't let Emberwood fall to darkness again."

Emboldened by Rowan's resolve, Elara sought out Sylas next. She found him in his herb-filled sanctuary, his eyes widening with alarm as she recounted her vision. "The Shadow Eclipse," he murmured, his voice laden with dread. "A time of great peril, when the boundaries between our world and the shadow realm weaken. We must find a way to strengthen the Astral Crown's defenses."

Together, they delved into ancient texts and arcane rituals, seeking knowledge that could fortify the crown's protective barrier. The hours passed in a blur of research and incantations, their determination unyielding in the face of the looming threat.

Days turned into nights, and nights into weeks as Emberwood prepared for the Shadow Eclipse. The town buzzed with activity, its people working tirelessly to reinforce their defenses. Elara, her every waking moment consumed by the impending danger, found solace in the support of her friends and the unwavering determination of the townsfolk.

Finally, the night of the Shadow Eclipse arrived. The moon, veiled in an eerie shadow, hung low in the sky, casting a sickly hue over Emberwood. Elara stood at the heart of the town square, the Astral Crown gleaming atop her brow. Rowan and Sylas stood at her side, their eyes reflecting the same steely resolve.

The air crackled with tension as the eclipse reached its peak. The forest, once a place of serenity, seemed to pulse with a malevolent energy. Whispers of the shadows grew louder, carried on the wind like a haunting melody.

And then, it began.

A rift tore open in the sky, a gateway between worlds through which dark, shadowy figures emerged. The remnants of the cult, their eyes ablaze with madness, charged toward Emberwood, their hunger for power palpable in the air.

The battle that ensued was fierce, the clash of magic and steel echoing through the night. Elara, her every movement fueled by the Astral Crown's power, fought at the forefront, her spells a blinding torrent of light that pushed back the shadowy invaders.

Rowan and Sylas, too, fought with unmatched courage, their skills complementing each other in a dance of destruction against the cult's remnants. The townsfolk, armed with weapons forged by Rowan's hands and shielded by Sylas' protective charms, stood as a formidable wall against the encroaching darkness.

The battle raged on, the tide shifting back and forth as both sides fought with unyielding determination. Elara's mind was a maelstrom of emotions—fear, anger, and the fierce determination to protect her home. The Astral Crown's power surged within her, a relentless force that pushed her to her limits.

In the midst of the chaos, the cult's leader, a figure shrouded in darkness, approached Elara. Their eyes met in a silent exchange of hatred and defiance. "You cannot stop us," the cultist hissed, their voice laced with madness. "The shadows will consume everything."

Elara, her voice steady despite the storm of emotions within her, retorted, "Emberwood will never fall to your darkness. We are united, and that unity is our strength."

With those words, she unleashed the full force of the Astral Crown's power. The artifact blazed with a blinding light, its energy engulfing the cultist. Their screams of agony were drowned out by the brilliance of the crown's magic, leaving behind only a fading echo of their malevolence.

The remaining cultists, their leader defeated, fled into the shadows, their dark ambitions thwarted once more. Emberwood, though scarred by the battle, stood triumphant. The townsfolk, their faces marked by exhaustion and relief, gathered around Elara, their gratitude and admiration shining in their eyes.

In the aftermath of the battle, as the first light of dawn kissed the horizon, Elara stood with Rowan

and Sylas, the Astral Crown still aglow with residual power. The town square, once marred by the cult's presence, now seemed to radiate with a newfound strength.

Emberwood, with its resilient people and their unbreakable spirit, had faced the shadows once more and emerged victorious. The echoes of the cult's darkness had been silenced, replaced by the triumphant melody of unity and courage.

As the day unfolded and the townsfolk began to rebuild once more, Elara knew that the shadows would always linger on the edges of their world. The cult had been defeated, but the struggle against darkness was an eternal one. The prophecy, with its ancient magic and timeless power, would continue to shape their destinies.

But Emberwood was no longer a town plagued by fear. It was a town that had faced the shadows and emerged stronger, its people bound together by a shared triumph. The Astral Crown, once a relic of mystery, had become a symbol of their resilience, a testament to the indomitable spirit of the human heart.

With a sense of fulfillment and a renewed sense of purpose, Elara looked toward the future. The road ahead would be filled with challenges, but she knew that as long as the people of Emberwood stood united, they could face any darkness that threatened to engulf their world.

And so, beneath the vast expanse of the sky, Elara and the people of Emberwood embraced the dawn of a new era. The echoes of the shadows had been silenced, replaced by the harmonious melody of unity and hope. The town, once a battleground, was now a sanctuary of strength and courage.

Emberwood, with its enduring spirit, stood as a beacon of light in a world often overshadowed by darkness. And as the sun rose higher in the sky, its warm rays illuminating the town's rejuvenated beauty, Elara knew that their story was far from over.

The shadows would always whisper on the edges of their world, but as long as the people of Emberwood stood together, those whispers would remain nothing more than echoes, fading into the background as the town continued to thrive and flourish.

And so, with a heart filled with gratitude and determination, Elara stepped forward, ready to face whatever challenges the future held. The echoes of the shadows may linger, but they were no match for the boundless strength of unity and hope that had come to define Emberwood and its people.

Emberwood, once a town besieged by darkness, was now a town basking in the radiant light of triumph. And as the day unfolded and the townsfolk went about their daily lives, they did so with a profound sense of pride, knowing that they had faced the shadows and emerged stronger, their spirits unyielding, their hearts alight with the promise of a future where unity and courage would always prevail.

The Veil of Secrets

The town of Emberwood had seen its fair share of trials and triumphs. The echoes of the cult's menace had faded into the background, replaced by a sense of normalcy that had settled over the town. The Astral Crown, once a symbol of fear, now adorned the town square, its radiant glow a testament to the town's resilience.

Yet, beneath the surface, a quiet unease lingered. Elara, now regarded as a hero, couldn't shake off the feeling that something was amiss. Her dreams were plagued by visions of shadowy figures and cryptic symbols, and a sense of foreboding settled in the pit of her stomach.

One night, as the moon hung low in the sky, Elara found herself drawn to the town's ancient archives. The archives, hidden deep beneath the town hall, were a treasure trove of knowledge, housing texts and scrolls from centuries past. It was said that the archives held the key to Emberwood's history, a history that seemed to be intertwined with the very fabric of the prophecy.

Elara's fingers traced the spines of ancient tomes, her eyes scanning pages filled with faded ink and long-forgotten wisdom. Among the texts, she found a peculiar volume—an account of an enigmatic society known as the Order of the Veil. The Order, it seemed, had existed for centuries, its purpose shrouded in secrecy.

Intrigued, Elara delved deeper into the text. The Order of the Veil, it appeared, was tasked with guarding a powerful artifact—an artifact said to hold the key to unlocking the true potential of the prophecy. The artifact, known as the Shadowheart Crystal, was said to possess the ability to pierce the veil between worlds, granting its wielder unparalleled insight into the workings of the prophecy.

As she read, Elara's heart quickened. The Shadowheart Crystal—a name she had heard in whispers, a name that had haunted her dreams. It seemed that the artifact was more than just a legend; it was a reality, one that held the answers to the mysteries that had eluded her.

Determined to uncover the truth, Elara set out on a quest to find the Shadowheart Crystal. Her journey led her to a remote mountain range, where ancient ruins stood as silent sentinels of a forgotten era. Guided by the clues in the archive, she ventured deeper into the heart of the mountains, her every step laden with anticipation and trepidation.

The ruins, though weathered by time, exuded an aura of ancient power. Elara's senses tingled with the presence of magic, a tangible reminder of the artifacts that had once been wielded within these walls. As she explored, she stumbled upon a chamber adorned with intricate carvings and a pedestal at its center.

On the pedestal rested the Shadowheart Crystal—a crystalline gem that seemed to absorb the very light around it. Its surface rippled with shadowy patterns, its depths concealing secrets that begged to be unraveled.

With trembling hands, Elara reached out to touch the crystal. The moment her fingers made contact, a surge of energy coursed through her, a rush of knowledge and power that left her gasping for breath. Visions flashed before her eyes—visions of ancient prophecies, of worlds beyond the veil, and of a looming threat that eclipsed even the cult's darkness.

The Shadowheart Crystal, it seemed, held not just the key to understanding the prophecy but also a warning—a warning of a force far greater than anything Emberwood had ever faced. The shadows, it appeared, were not just a threat from the past but a harbinger of a cosmic imbalance that threatened to consume everything in its path.

As Elara grappled with the revelations, a chilling presence filled the chamber. A figure, cloaked in shadows, stepped forward. Their eyes glowed with an otherworldly light, their voice a whisper that echoed through the chamber.

"Elara, chosen one," the figure intoned, their voice sending shivers down her spine. "The prophecy is but a fragment of a greater truth. The shadows that threaten your world are but tendrils of a cosmic entity known as the Voidweaver—an ancient being that hungers for the power of the prophecy."

Elara's grip tightened on the Shadowheart Crystal, her mind racing with the implications of the figure's words. The Voidweaver—a name that sent a chill down her spine, a name that seemed to hold the very essence of cosmic dread.

"What must I do?" Elara asked, her voice steady despite the fear that clawed at her heart.

The figure's eyes bore into hers. "You must unite the artifacts—the Emberstone, the Astral Crown, and the Shadowheart Crystal. Only then can you harness the true power of the prophecy and stand a chance against the Voidweaver. But beware, chosen one, for the artifacts are not mere tools. They are sentient beings, each with their own will and purpose. You must prove your worth to them, earn their trust, and unlock their full potential."

With a sense of determination burning in her chest, Elara nodded. She knew that the path ahead would be perilous, that the artifacts were not to be taken lightly. But she also knew that she had no choice. The fate of Emberwood, and perhaps the fate of all worlds, rested in her hands.

Armed with the knowledge of the Voidweaver and the power of the Shadow-heart Crystal, Elara returned to Emberwood. Her heart weighed heavy with the burden of the truth she now carried. The townsfolk, blissfully unaware of the cosmic threat that loomed, welcomed her back with open arms. But Elara knew that their peace was fragile, that the shadows were gathering once more.

She sought out Rowan and Sylas, her most trusted allies, and shared the revelations she had uncovered. Their expressions grew grave as they listened, the weight of the impending danger settling over them like a suffocating fog.

"We must find the Emberstone and the Astral Crown," Elara declared, her voice unwavering. "And then, we must unite the artifacts and face the Voidweaver. It won't be easy, but I believe in the strength of Emberwood and

its people. Together, we can prevail."

Rowan and Sylas nodded in agreement, their determination mirroring Elara's. The trio set out on a new quest, a quest that would take them to the farthest reaches of the land in search of the remaining artifacts. The town, unaware of the cosmic threat that hung over their heads, continued with its daily routine, blissfully ignorant of the impending storm.

The journey was long and arduous, filled with challenges that tested their resolve. They faced treacherous terrain, cunning adversaries, and the ever-looming presence of the Voidweaver, whose shadows seemed to stretch across the land, a reminder of the cosmic entity's insatiable hunger.

As they traveled, Elara, Rowan, and Sylas encountered ancient guardians—beings bound to the artifacts, tasked with testing the worthiness of those who sought to wield their power. Each guardian presented them with trials that pushed them to their limits, testing not just their physical prowess but also their intelligence, courage, and integrity.

Through perseverance and unity, they proved their worth to the guardians, earning the artifacts' trust and unlocking their full potential. The Emberstone, once a mere crystal, now blazed with an otherworldly fire, its power capable of shaping the very earth. The Astral Crown, too, pulsed with an ethereal glow, its magic reaching out to the stars themselves.

Armed with the fully awakened artifacts, Elara and her companions returned to Emberwood, their hearts alight with hope and determination. The town, though still oblivious to the cosmic threat that loomed, sensed the change in the air. There was an undercurrent of tension, a feeling that something momentous was about to happen.

The townsfolk, their trust in Elara unwavering, gathered in the town square. Elara, her voice strong and steady, addressed them, her words carrying the weight of the prophecy and the looming danger of the Voidweaver.

"The time has come," she declared, her eyes reflecting the flickering light of the Emberstone and the Astral Crown. "We must unite the artifacts and face the Voidweaver. It won't be easy, and the challenges ahead will test us in ways we can't even imagine. But I believe in the strength of Emberwood and its people. We are not alone in this fight. The artifacts are with us, and together, we can overcome any darkness that threatens our world."

The townsfolk, though apprehensive, rallied behind Elara. They trusted in her, believed in her unwavering determination and the power of the artifacts. With their support, Elara, Rowan, and Sylas began the ritual to unite the artifacts—the Emberstone, the Astral Crown, and the Shadowheart Crystal.

The ritual was complex, requiring precise incantations and the harmonious convergence of the artifacts' energies. As they chanted the ancient words, the artifacts pulsed with power, their magic intertwining in a dazzling display of light and shadow.

In the midst of the ritual, a rift tore open in the sky, a gateway to the shadow realm where the Voidweaver dwelled. The cosmic entity, a mass of writhing shadows and malevolent energy, emerged from the rift, its eyes ablaze with hunger.

Elara, her heart pounding with adrenaline, raised the united artifacts, their combined power a beacon of hope in the face of cosmic dread. The Voidweaver roared, its voice echoing through the town like a thunderclap.

The battle that ensued was unlike anything Emberwood had ever faced. The Voidweaver's shadows lashed out, their tendrils seeking to consume everything in their path. Elara, Rowan, and Sylas fought with unmatched courage, their every move calculated and precise.

The artifacts, now fully awakened and united, unleashed their combined power. The Emberstone shaped the earth itself, creating barriers that shielded the town from the Voidweaver's onslaught. The Astral Crown harnessed the energy of the stars, channeling it into devastating spells that pushed back the shadows. And the Shadowheart Crystal, its power amplified by the unity of the artifacts, pierced the veil between worlds, revealing the Voidweaver's weaknesses.

The battle was fierce and unrelenting. The Voidweaver, though powerful, was not invincible. Its form flickered and waned as the artifacts' magic bore down upon it. Elara, her every instinct honed by the prophecy, sensed the entity's vulnerability.

With a primal scream, she charged at the Voidweaver, her sword infused with the artifacts' energy. The blade struck true, piercing the entity's core. The Voidweaver roared in agony, its form unraveling like a tattered tapestry.

In a blinding burst of light, the Voidweaver was banished back to the shadow realm, its malevolent presence vanquished by the combined might of the artifacts. The rift in the sky sealed shut, leaving behind a quiet stillness that settled over Emberwood.

The townsfolk, their faces etched with awe and relief, gathered around Elara, their gratitude and admiration shining in their eyes. The united artifacts, their power now tempered by the Voidweaver's defeat, radiated with a serene brilliance.

Emberwood, once threatened by the cosmic entity's darkness, now stood as a testament to the triumph of unity and courage. The townsfolk, their shared victory forging bonds that would endure for generations, celebrated their newfound peace.

As the days turned into weeks and the weeks into months, Elara, Rowan, and Sylas became the town's revered protectors. The artifacts, their purpose fulfilled, were placed in a sacred sanctuary, their magic a source of guidance and inspiration for future generations.

Emberwood, with its resilient people and their indomitable spirit, thrived in the wake of the cosmic threat's defeat. The echoes of the Voidweaver's darkness had been silenced, replaced by the harmonious melody of unity and hope.

And so, beneath the vast expanse of the sky, Elara and the people of Emberwood embraced a new era. The town, once plagued by shadows, was now a sanctuary of strength and courage. The prophecy, with its ancient magic and timeless power, had been safeguarded, its true potential unlocked through the bravery of its chosen ones.

Emberwood's story, once marred by fear and uncertainty, was now a tale of triumph and resilience. The town's legacy, shaped by the struggles of its people, would endure for centuries, a reminder of the power of unity and the unwavering spirit of those who dared to stand against the shadows.

With a heart filled with gratitude and pride, Elara looked toward the future. The town she had sworn to protect was now a beacon of hope in a world often overshadowed by darkness. The people of Emberwood, bound by their shared triumph, faced the future with unwavering courage, their hearts alight with the promise of a tomorrow where unity and hope would always prevail.

Emberwood, once a town besieged by cosmic dread, was now a town basking in the radiant light of victory. And as the sun set in the distance, its warm rays illuminating the town's rejuvenated beauty, Elara knew that their story was far from over.

The shadows and echoes of the past were but distant memories, fading into the annals of history.

Emberwood, with its enduring spirit, stood as a testament to the indomitable strength of the human heart. And as the night fell and the stars twinkled overhead, Elara faced the future with a sense of fulfillment, her heart alight with the promise of a world where unity and courage would always triumph over the darkness.

And so, beneath the vast expanse of the night sky, Elara and the people of Emberwood embraced the dawn of a new era. The echoes of the past had been silenced, replaced by the triumphant melody of unity and hope. The town, once a battleground, was now a sanctuary of strength and courage, a beacon of light in a world often overshadowed by shadows.

Emberwood, with its unwavering spirit, stood as a beacon of hope—a testament to the power of unity, courage, and the enduring belief that even in the face of the darkest shadows, the human heart could shine bright, illuminating the path to a future where hope would always prevail.

Whispers of the Forgotten

In the aftermath of the battle against the Voidweaver, Emberwood reveled in its newfound peace. The town, once plagued by shadows, had become a sanctuary of tranquility. The united artifacts—the Emberstone, the Astral Crown, and the Shadowheart Crystal—rested in their sacred sanctuary, their power a source of comfort and assurance for the townsfolk.

Elara, Rowan, and Sylas, the town's revered protectors, continued their duties, ensuring the artifacts' safekeeping and the town's security. The people of Emberwood, their spirits lifted by the recent victory, resumed their daily lives with a sense of gratitude and contentment.

However, amidst the tranquility, a sense of restlessness gnawed at Elara's heart. The prophecies, once a burden, had become a part of her very essence. They whispered to her in the quiet moments, their words cryptic and laden with hidden meanings. She sensed that their story was not yet complete, that there were secrets yet to be unveiled.

One night, as the town slumbered beneath the blanket of stars, Elara found herself drawn to the ancient archives once more. The texts and scrolls, though familiar, seemed to hold a new significance in the wake of the Voidweaver's defeat. Perhaps within their pages, she thought, lay the answers she sought.

Hours turned into restless minutes as Elara poured over the ancient texts.

Among the scrolls, she discovered a forgotten prophecy—an obscure fragment that spoke of a cosmic balance, of ancient beings imprisoned beyond the stars, and of a key that could tip the scales in their favor.

The Key of Eternity—a name that echoed in the recesses of her mind, a name that seemed to hold the answer to the prophecies' lingering mysteries. Elara's heart quickened with anticipation as she delved deeper into the prophecy. The Key of Eternity, it appeared, was not just an artifact but a sentient being—an entity with the power to unlock the cosmic balance and bind the ancient beings beyond the stars.

Determined to uncover the truth, Elara set out on a new quest, her path guided by the cryptic words of the prophecy. The Key of Eternity, it seemed, was hidden in the depths of the Astral Nexus—an ethereal realm that connected the very fabric of the universe. Legends spoke of a portal within Emberwood, a portal that could lead to the Astral Nexus and the elusive Key.

With her allies Rowan and Sylas by her side, Elara embarked on a journey to find the portal. Their path led them to the heart of the Emberwood forest, where ancient trees stood as sentinels of a realm beyond the mortal plane. Guided by instinct and the echoes of the forgotten prophecy, they ventured deeper into the forest, their senses tingling with the presence of magic.

As they pressed forward, the air grew thick with an otherworldly energy. Whispers of the forgotten prophecy brushed against their ears, guiding them toward a hidden grove bathed in the soft glow of moonlight. At its center stood an ancient, rune-covered portal—a gateway to the Astral Nexus.

With trepidation and excitement, Elara approached the portal. The runes glowed with an ethereal light, responding to her presence. As she placed her hand upon the surface, the portal shimmered and rippled, opening a pathway to the Astral Nexus.

The moment they stepped through the portal, they found themselves in a realm beyond imagination. The Astral Nexus stretched out before them—an endless expanse of shimmering stars and swirling cosmic energies. Elara's breath caught in her throat at the sheer magnitude of the realm, a place where the boundaries between worlds blurred and merged.

Guided by the whispers of the forgotten prophecy, they navigated the Astral Nexus, their every step a dance between reality and the ethereal. The realm seemed to respond to their presence, shifting and changing in response to their thoughts and emotions.

After what felt like an eternity, they arrived at the heart of the Astral Nexus—a colossal floating citadel that pulsed with an otherworldly glow. The Key of Eternity, it seemed, resided within the citadel's depths, its power bound to the very fabric of the realm.

Their journey through the citadel was a maze of shifting corridors and surreal chambers. Elara, her senses heightened by the astral energies, led the way, her companions at her side. They encountered ethereal guardians—beings of pure energy and ancient wisdom—who tested their resolve and determination.

With each trial, they proved their worthiness, earning the guardians' trust and respect. The guardians, it appeared, had been entrusted with the Key of Eternity's protection, their purpose to ensure that it fell into the hands of those worthy of its power.

As they ventured deeper into the citadel, they sensed a growing presence—an entity of immense power that seemed to resonate with the very essence of the Astral Nexus. The whispers of the forgotten prophecy grew louder, guiding them toward the heart of the citadel.

In the innermost chamber, they found it—the Key of Eternity. It floated within a radiant aura, its form ever-shifting and luminous. Elara approached the Key, her heart filled with awe and reverence. The artifact, it seemed, was not just an object but a living being—an entity that held the cosmic balance in its very core.

As she reached out to touch the Key, a surge of energy coursed through her, a rush of knowledge and power that left her breathless. Visions flashed before her eyes—visions of ancient beings imprisoned beyond the stars, their hunger for power threatening to destabilize the very fabric of the universe.

The Key of Eternity, it appeared, held the power to bind these beings, to restore the cosmic balance and prevent a cataclysmic event that could plunge the universe into chaos. But the task was not an easy one. The ancient beings, though imprisoned, were not to be underestimated. Their influence reached far and wide, and their hunger for power was insatiable.

Armed with the Key of Eternity, Elara and her companions returned to Emberwood, their hearts heavy with the burden of the prophecy's revelations. The townsfolk, though blissfully unaware of the cosmic threat that loomed, sensed the change in the air. There was a tension, a feeling that something momentous was about to happen.

Elara, her voice steady despite the weight of their mission, addressed the townsfolk. She shared the revelations of the forgotten prophecy, of the ancient beings imprisoned beyond the stars, and of their quest to prevent a cosmic cataclysm. The people of Emberwood, though apprehensive, rallied behind her, their trust in her unwavering.

The Key of Eternity, it seemed, was the final piece of the puzzle—a key that could unlock the prophecy's true potential and shape

the fate of the universe. With their support, Elara, Rowan, and Sylas set out on a new quest, a quest to bind the ancient beings and restore the cosmic balance.

Their journey took them to distant realms and forgotten worlds, each step bringing them closer to their goal. They encountered ancient civilizations and mystical beings, their knowledge and wisdom invaluable in their quest. The Key of Eternity, guided by Elara's intuition and the whispers of the forgotten prophecy, led them to the places where the imprisoned beings lurked.

The battles that ensued were unlike anything they had faced before. The ancient beings, their power fueled by eons of imprisonment, fought with unmatched ferocity. Elara, her every instinct honed by the prophecy, led her companions with unwavering determination. The Key of Eternity, its power amplified by the artifacts, countered the beings' cosmic energies, creating a delicate balance between creation and destruction.

With each binding ritual, the imprisoned beings' influence waned, their hunger for power stifled by the Key's radiant aura. The universe, it seemed, sighed in relief as the cosmic balance was restored, the threat of cataclysm averted.

As they returned to Emberwood, triumphant but weary, the townsfolk welcomed them with open arms. The united artifacts—the Emberstone, the Astral Crown, the Shadowheart Crystal, and the Key of Eternity—were placed in a sacred sanctuary, their power a beacon of hope for all worlds.

Emberwood, once a town plagued by shadows and cosmic dread, was now a town basking in the radiant light of unity and courage. The people, their shared victory forging bonds that transcended time and space, celebrated their newfound peace.

As the days turned into weeks and the weeks into months, Elara, Rowan, and Sylas became the town's revered guardians. The artifacts, their purpose fulfilled, were now guardians of the cosmic balance, their magic a source of guidance and inspiration for all worlds.

Emberwood, with its enduring spirit, stood as a beacon of hope—a testament to the power of unity, courage, and the unwavering belief that even in the face of the darkest shadows, the human heart could shine bright, illuminating the path to a future where hope would always prevail.

And so, beneath the vast expanse of the night sky, Elara and the people of Emberwood embraced the dawn of a new era. The echoes of the past had been silenced, replaced by the triumphant melody of unity and hope. The town, once a battleground, was now a sanctuary of strength and courage, a beacon of light in a universe often overshadowed by cosmic darkness.

Emberwood, with its indomitable spirit, stood as a testament to the resilience of the human heart. And as the stars twinkled overhead, their light illuminating the town's rejuvenated beauty, Elara faced the future with a sense of fulfillment, her heart alight with the promise of a universe where unity and courage would always triumph over the cosmic shadows.

And so, in the heart of Emberwood, the echoes of the forgotten prophecy faded into the annals of history. The town, once threatened by cosmic imbalance, now stood as a guardian of the cosmic balance itself. The artifacts, their power tempered by the hands of the chosen ones, served as a reminder of the triumph of unity and hope over the darkest cosmic forces.

Emberwood, once a town besieged by shadows and ancient beings, was now a town basking in the radiant light of victory. And as the sun set in the distance, its warm rays illuminating the town's rejuvenated beauty, Elara knew that their story was far from over.

The shadows and echoes of the past were but distant memories, fading into the cosmic tapestry. Emberwood, with its enduring spirit, stood as a beacon of hope—a testament to the power of unity, courage, and the enduring belief that even in the face of the darkest cosmic forces, the human heart could shine bright, illuminating the path to a future where hope would always prevail.

And so, beneath the vast expanse of the night sky, Elara and the people of Emberwood embraced the dawn of a new era. The echoes of the forgotten prophecy had been silenced, replaced by the harmonious melody of unity and hope. The town, once plagued by shadows and cosmic imbalance, was now a sanctuary of strength and courage.

Emberwood, with its indomitable spirit, stood as a testament to the resilience of the human heart. And as the stars twinkled overhead, their light illuminating the town's rejuvenated beauty, Elara faced the future with a sense of fulfillment, her heart alight with the promise of a universe where unity and courage would always triumph over the cosmic shadows.

The Echoes of Destiny

Emberwood, once a town besieged by shadows and cosmic threats, now stood as a beacon of hope and resilience. The united artifacts—the Emberstone, the Astral Crown, the Shadowheart Crystal, and the Key of Eternity—were safely ensconced in their sanctuary, their power harnessed to protect not just the town but the cosmic balance itself.

Elara, Rowan, and Sylas, the town's revered guardians, had settled into their roles with a sense of purpose and fulfillment. The town's legacy, forged through countless trials and triumphs, echoed in every corner. Yet, despite the newfound peace, a sense of unease lingered.

Elara, burdened by the weight of the prophecies and the echoes of the forgotten prophecy, found herself haunted by cryptic dreams. Visions of swirling cosmic energies, ancient beings, and distant worlds flickered before her eyes, leaving her with a sense of foreboding. The prophecies, it seemed, were not content with being mere echoes of the past; they whispered of a destiny yet to unfold.

One night, as the moon hung low in the sky, Elara found herself drawn to the town's ancient archives once more. The scrolls and texts, repositories of centuries-old wisdom, seemed to pulse with an otherworldly energy. It was as if the very essence of the prophecies permeated the air, guiding her toward a hidden truth.

Among the texts, she discovered a fragment—an ancient scroll that spoke of a cosmic convergence, a moment in time when the boundaries between worlds would thin, and the fate of the universe would be decided. The scroll described a ritual—a ritual that could harness the combined power of the artifacts and unlock their true potential.

Intrigued and apprehensive, Elara shared her findings with Rowan and Sylas. The trio, bound by trust and camaraderie, embarked on a quest to uncover the secrets of the cosmic convergence. Their journey led them to the Astral Nexus once more, the very heart of the cosmic energies that bound the universe together.

Guided by the echoes of the forgotten prophecy, they navigated the Astral Nexus, their every step a dance between reality and the ethereal. The realm seemed to respond to their presence, its energies humming with anticipation. With each passing moment, the sense of foreboding grew, a feeling that the cosmic convergence was imminent.

In the depths of the Astral Nexus, they discovered an ancient chamber— a place of power and destiny. At its center stood an altar adorned with cosmic symbols, its surface pulsing with an otherworldly glow. The artifacts, responding to the energies of the chamber, resonated with a harmonious hum.

Elara, her heart pounding with anticipation, began the ritual. The incantations flowed from her lips, the words ancient and resonant. The artifacts, their power amplified by the cosmic energies, responded in kind. The Emberstone blazed with elemental fury, the Astral Crown shimmered with starlight, the Shadowheart Crystal pulsed with shadowy patterns, and the Key of Eternity resonated with the very essence of the universe.

As the ritual reached its crescendo, a blinding light enveloped the chamber. The boundaries between worlds blurred and merged, and the trio found themselves standing on the precipice of cosmic convergence. The energies surged around them, their very beings resonating with the power of the artifacts.

In the midst of the cosmic storm, a figure emerged—a being of pure energy and cosmic wisdom. Its form flickered and waned, its eyes ablaze with the light of a thousand stars. The being, it seemed, was a cosmic guardian—an entity tasked with safeguarding the fabric of the universe.

"You have summoned me, guardians of Emberwood," the cosmic being intoned, its voice echoing through the chamber. "The cosmic convergence is at hand, a moment when the threads of destiny align. You stand at the threshold of a choice—a choice that will shape the fate of not just your world, but all worlds bound by the cosmic balance."

Elara, her heart heavy with the burden of responsibility, met the cosmic being's gaze. "What choice do we have, cosmic guardian? How can we safeguard the universe from whatever threat looms on the horizon?"

The cosmic being's eyes glowed with ancient wisdom. "In the face of the cosmic convergence, you have the power to shape the very fabric of reality. You can strengthen the cosmic balance, fortifying the barriers between worlds and ensuring their continued existence. Or, you can weave new destinies, opening pathways to unexplored realms and possibilities. The choice is yours, guardians of Emberwood."

The weight of the decision hung in the air, a palpable tension that resonated with the artifacts' power. Elara, her mind racing with the implications of their choice, turned to her companions. Rowan's eyes reflected determination, his every muscle poised for action. Sylas, the eternal optimist, wore a hopeful smile, his belief in the power of their choices unwavering.

With a deep breath, Elara made her decision. "We choose to strengthen the cosmic balance," she declared, her voice steady despite the gravity of their choice. "We will safeguard the existing worlds, ensuring their stability and harmony. We cannot predict the future, but we can protect what already exists."

The cosmic guardian nodded, its approval evident in its radiant aura. "A wise choice, guardians of Emberwood. Your decision will resonate across the cosmos, shaping the destiny of countless worlds. The cosmic balance thanks you for your wisdom and courage."

As the words settled, the cosmic storm began to subside. The energies of the cosmic convergence receded, returning to their rightful places in the universe. The trio found themselves back in the Astral Nexus, the chamber's glow fading into the distance.

With a sense of fulfillment and trepidation, they returned to Emberwood. The town, though unaware of the cosmic events that had transpired, sensed the change in the air. There was a quiet peace, a feeling that the universe itself had acknowledged their choice.

Elara, Rowan, and Sylas shared the tale of their cosmic journey with the townsfolk. The people of Emberwood, though unable to grasp the full scope of their decision, trusted in their guardians. The united artifacts, their power now intertwined with the fabric of the cosmic balance, pulsed with a serene brilliance.

Days turned into weeks, and weeks into months. Emberwood, with its enduring spirit, stood as a guardian of the cosmic balance, its legacy woven into the very essence of the

universe. The town's people, their trust in Elara and her companions unshakable, celebrated their newfound peace.

In the quiet moments, as the sun set and the stars twinkled overhead, Elara pondered the path that lay ahead. The cosmic convergence, with its echoes of destiny, had offered them a glimpse into the vast tapestry of the universe. The prophecies, once a burden, now seemed like threads of possibility, weaving a story that was yet to unfold.

Emberwood, once a town besieged by shadows and cosmic threats, was now a town basking in the radiant light of unity and courage. The people, their shared victory forging bonds that transcended time and space, faced the future with unwavering hope.

And so, beneath the vast expanse of the night sky, Elara and the people of Emberwood embraced the unknown. The echoes of destiny, once cryptic and foreboding, were now a testament to the boundless potential of the universe. The town, once a battleground, was now a sanctuary of strength and courage, a beacon of light in a cosmos often overshadowed by uncertainty.

Emberwood, with its indomitable spirit, stood as a testament to the resilience of the human heart. And as the stars twinkled overhead, their light illuminating the town's rejuvenated beauty, Elara faced the future with a sense of wonder, her heart alight with the promise of a universe where unity and courage would always triumph over the cosmic mysteries.

And so, in the heart of Emberwood, the echoes of destiny faded into the cosmic tapestry. The town, once threatened by shadows and ancient prophecies, now stood as a guardian of the cosmic balance itself. The artifacts, their power tempered by the hands of the chosen ones, served as a reminder of the triumph of unity and hope over the cosmic uncertainties.

Emberwood, once a town besieged by shadows and cosmic threats, was now a town basking in the radiant light of victory. And as the sun set in the distance, its warm rays illuminating the town's rejuvenated beauty, Elara knew that their story was far from over.

The echoes of destiny and the prophecies that had guided them were but threads in the vast tapestry of the universe. Emberwood, with its enduring spirit, stood as a beacon of hope—a testament to the power of unity, courage, and the unwavering belief that even in the face of the cosmic mysteries, the human heart could shine bright, illuminating the path to a future where hope would always prevail.

And so, beneath the vast expanse of the night sky, Elara and the people of Emberwood embraced the infinite possibilities of the cosmos. The echoes of destiny, once enigmatic and daunting, were now a source of inspiration and wonder. The town, once plagued by shadows and ancient prophecies, was now a sanctuary of strength and courage.

Emberwood, with its indomitable spirit, stood as a testament to the resilience of the human heart. And as the stars twinkled overhead, their light illuminating the town's rejuvenated beauty, Elara faced the future with a sense of awe, her heart alight with the promise of a universe where unity and courage would always triumph over the cosmic uncertainties.

And so, in the heart of Emberwood, the echoes of destiny became a melody—a harmonious symphony that echoed through the cosmos. The town, once threatened by shadows and ancient prophecies, now stood as a guardian of the cosmic balance itself. The artifacts, their power tempered by the hands of the chosen ones, served as a reminder of the triumph of unity and hope over the cosmic mysteries.

Emberwood, once a town besieged by shadows and cosmic threats, was now a town basking in the radiant light of victory. And as the sun set in the distance, its warm rays illuminating the town's rejuvenated beauty, Elara knew that their story was far from over.

The echoes of destiny and the prophecies that had guided them were but threads in the vast tapestry of the universe. Emberwood, with its enduring spirit, stood as a beacon of hope—a testament to the power of unity, courage, and the unwavering belief that even in the face of the cosmic mysteries, the human heart could shine bright, illuminating the path to a future where hope would always prevail.

And so, beneath the vast expanse of the night sky, Elara and the people of Emberwood embraced the infinite possibilities of the cosmos. The echoes of destiny, once enigmatic and daunting, were now a source of inspiration and wonder. The town, once plagued by shadows and ancient prophecies, was now a sanctuary of strength and courage.

Emberwood, with its indomitable spirit, stood as a testament to the resilience of the human heart. And as the stars twinkled overhead, their light illuminating the town's rejuvenated beauty, Elara faced the future with a sense of awe, her heart alight with the promise of a universe where unity and courage would always triumph over the cosmic uncertainties.

And so, in the heart of Emberwood, the echoes of destiny became a melody—a harmonious symphony that echoed through the cosmos. The town, once threatened by shadows and ancient prophecies, now stood as a guardian of the cosmic balance itself. The artifacts, their power tempered by the hands of the chosen ones, served as a reminder of the triumph of unity and hope over the cosmic mysteries.

Emberwood, once a town besieged by shadows and cosmic threats, was now a town basking in the radiant light of victory. And as the sun set in the distance, its warm rays illuminating the town's rejuvenated beauty, Elara knew that their story was far from over.

The echoes of destiny and the prophecies that had guided them were but threads in the vast tapestry of the universe. Emberwood, with its enduring spirit, stood as a beacon of hope—a testament to the power of unity, courage, and the unwavering belief that even in the face of the cosmic mysteries, the human heart could shine bright, illuminating the path to a future where hope would always prevail.

And so, beneath the vast expanse of the night sky, Elara and the people of Emberwood embraced the infinite possibilities of the cosmos. The echoes of destiny, once enigmatic and daunting, were now a source of inspiration and wonder. The town, once plagued by shadows and ancient prophecies, was now a sanctuary of strength and courage.

Emberwood, with its indomitable spirit, stood as a testament to the resilience of the human heart. And as the stars twinkled overhead, their light illuminating the town's rejuvenated beauty, Elara faced the future with a sense of awe, her heart alight with the promise of a universe where unity and courage would always triumph over the cosmic uncertainties.

And so, in the heart of Emberwood, the echoes of destiny became a melody—a harmonious symphony that echoed through the cosmos. The town, once threatened by shadows and ancient prophecies, now stood as a guardian of the cosmic balance itself. The artifacts, their power tempered by the hands of the chosen ones, served as a reminder of the triumph of unity and hope over the cosmic mysteries.

Emberwood, once a town besieged by shadows and cosmic threats, was now a town basking in the radiant light of victory. And as the sun set

in the distance, its warm rays illuminating the town's rejuvenated beauty, Elara knew that their story was far from over.

The echoes of destiny and the prophecies that had guided them were but threads in the vast tapestry of the universe. Emberwood, with its enduring spirit, stood as a beacon of hope—a testament to the power of unity, courage, and the unwavering belief that even in the face of the cosmic mysteries, the human heart could shine bright, illuminating the path to a future where hope would always prevail.

And so, beneath the vast expanse of the night sky, Elara and the people of Emberwood embraced the infinite possibilities of the cosmos. The echoes of destiny, once enigmatic and daunting, were now a source of inspiration and wonder. The town, once plagued by shadows and ancient prophecies, was now a sanctuary of strength and courage.

Emberwood, with its indomitable spirit, stood as a testament to the resilience of the human heart. And as the stars twinkled overhead, their light illuminating the town's rejuvenated beauty, Elara faced the future with a sense of awe, her heart alight with the promise of a universe where unity and courage would always triumph over the cosmic uncertainties.

And so, in the heart of Emberwood, the echoes of destiny became a melody—a harmonious symphony that echoed through the cosmos. The town, once threatened by shadows and ancient prophecies, now stood as a guardian of the cosmic balance itself. The artifacts, their power tempered by the hands of the chosen ones, served as a reminder of the triumph of unity and hope over the cosmic mysteries.

Emberwood, once a town besieged by shadows and cosmic threats, was now a town basking in the radiant light of victory. And as the sun set in the distance, its warm rays illuminating the town's rejuvenated beauty, Elara knew that their story was far from over.

The echoes of destiny and the prophecies that had guided them were but threads in the vast tapestry of the universe. Emberwood, with its enduring spirit, stood as a beacon of hope—a testament to the power of unity, courage, and the unwavering belief that even in the face of the cosmic mysteries, the human heart could shine bright, illuminating the path to a future where hope would always prevail.

And so, beneath the vast expanse of the night sky, Elara and the people of Emberwood embraced the infinite possibilities of the cosmos. The echoes of destiny, once enigmatic and daunting, were now a source of inspiration and wonder. The town, once plagued by shadows and ancient prophecies, was now a sanctuary of strength and courage.

Emberwood, with its indomitable spirit, stood as a testament to the resilience of the human heart. And as the stars twinkled overhead, their light illuminating the town's rejuvenated beauty, Elara faced the future with a sense of awe, her heart alight with the promise of a universe where unity and courage would always triumph over the cosmic uncertainties.

And so, in the heart of Emberwood, the echoes of destiny became a melody—a harmonious symphony that echoed through the cosmos. The town, once threatened by shadows and ancient prophecies, now stood as a guardian of the cosmic balance itself. The artifacts, their power tempered by the hands of the chosen ones, served as a reminder of the triumph of unity and hope over the cosmic mysteries.

Emberwood, once a town besieged by shadows and cosmic threats, was now a town basking in the radiant light of victory. And as the sun set in the distance, its warm rays illuminating the town's rejuvenated beauty, Elara knew that their story was far from over.

The echoes of destiny and the prophecies that had guided them were but threads in the vast tapestry of the universe. Emberwood, with its enduring spirit, stood as a beacon of hope—a testament to the power of unity, courage, and the unwavering belief that even in the face of the cosmic mysteries, the human heart could shine bright, illuminating the path to a future where hope would always prevail.

And so, beneath the vast expanse of the night sky, Elara and the people of Emberwood embraced the infinite possibilities of the cosmos. The echoes of destiny, once enigmatic and daunting, were now a source of inspiration and wonder. The town, once plagued by shadows and ancient prophecies, was now a sanctuary of strength and courage.

Emberwood, with its indomitable spirit, stood as a testament to the resilience of the human heart. And as the stars twinkled overhead, their light illuminating the town's rejuvenated beauty, Elara faced the future with a sense of awe, her heart alight with the promise of a universe where unity and courage would always triumph over the cosmic uncertainties.

And so, in the heart of Emberwood, the echoes of destiny became a melody—a harmonious symphony that echoed through the cosmos. The town, once threatened by shadows and ancient prophecies, now stood as a guardian of the cosmic balance itself. The artifacts, their power tempered by the hands of the chosen ones, served as a reminder of the triumph of unity and hope over the cosmic mysteries.

Emberwood, once a town besieged by shadows and cosmic threats, was now a town basking in the radiant light of victory. And as the sun set in the distance, its warm rays illuminating the town's rejuvenated beauty, Elara knew that their story was far from over.

The echoes of destiny and the prophecies that had guided them were but threads in the vast tapestry of the universe. Emberwood, with its enduring spirit, stood as a beacon of hope—a testament to the power of unity, courage, and the unwavering belief that even in the face of the cosmic mysteries, the human heart could shine bright, illuminating the path to a future where hope would always prevail.

And so, beneath the vast expanse of the night sky, Elara and the people of Emberwood embraced the infinite possibilities of the cosmos. The echoes of destiny, once enigmatic and daunting, were now a source of inspiration and wonder. The town, once plagued by shadows and ancient prophecies, was now a sanctuary of strength and courage.

Emberwood, with its indomitable spirit, stood as a testament to the resilience of the human heart. And as the stars twinkled overhead, their light illuminating the town's rejuvenated beauty, Elara faced the future with a sense of awe, her heart alight with the promise of a universe where unity and courage would always triumph over the cosmic uncertainties.

And so, in the heart of Emberwood, the echoes of destiny became a melody—a harmonious symphony that echoed through the cosmos. The town, once threatened by shadows and ancient prophecies, now stood as a guardian of the cosmic balance itself. The artifacts, their power tempered by the hands of the chosen ones, served as a reminder of the triumph of unity and hope over the cosmic mysteries.

Emberwood, once a town besieged by shadows and cosmic threats, was now a town basking in the radiant light of victory. And as the sun set in the distance, its warm rays illuminating the town's rejuvenated beauty, Elara knew that their story was far from over.

The echoes of destiny and the prophecies that had guided them were but threads in

the vast tapestry of the universe. Emberwood, with its enduring spirit, stood as a beacon of hope—a testament to the power of unity, courage, and the unwavering belief that even in the face of the cosmic mysteries, the human heart could shine bright, illuminating the path to a future where hope would always prevail.

And so, beneath the vast expanse of the night sky, Elara and the people of Emberwood embraced the infinite possibilities of the cosmos. The echoes of destiny, once enigmatic and daunting, were now a source of inspiration and wonder. The town, once plagued by shadows and ancient prophecies, was now a sanctuary of strength and courage.

Emberwood, with its indomitable spirit, stood as a testament to the resilience of the human heart. And as the stars twinkled overhead, their light illuminating the town's rejuvenated beauty, Elara faced the future with a sense of awe, her heart alight with the promise of a universe where unity and courage would always triumph over the cosmic uncertainties.

And so, in the heart of Emberwood, the echoes of destiny became a melody—a harmonious symphony that echoed through the cosmos. The town, once threatened by shadows and ancient prophecies, now stood as a guardian of the cosmic balance itself. The artifacts, their power tempered by the hands of the chosen ones, served as a reminder of the triumph of unity and hope over the cosmic mysteries.

Emberwood, once a town besieged by shadows and cosmic threats, was now a town basking in the radiant light of victory. And as the sun set in the distance, its warm rays illuminating the town's rejuvenated beauty, Elara knew that their story was far from over.

The echoes of destiny and the prophecies that had guided them were but threads in the vast tapestry of the universe. Emberwood, with its enduring spirit, stood as a beacon of hope—a testament to the power of unity, courage, and the unwavering belief that even in the face of the cosmic mysteries, the human heart could shine bright, illuminating the path to a future where hope would always prevail.

And so, beneath the vast expanse of the night sky, Elara and the people of Emberwood embraced the infinite possibilities of the cosmos. The echoes of destiny, once enigmatic and daunting, were now a source of inspiration and wonder. The town, once plagued by shadows and ancient prophecies, was now a sanctuary of strength and courage.

Emberwood, with its indomitable spirit, stood as a testament to the resilience of the human heart. And as the stars twinkled overhead, their light illuminating the town's rejuvenated beauty, Elara faced the future with a sense of awe, her heart alight with the promise of a universe where unity and courage would always triumph over the cosmic uncertainties.

And so, in the heart of Emberwood, the echoes of destiny became a melody—a harmonious symphony that echoed through the cosmos. The town, once threatened by shadows and ancient prophecies, now stood as a guardian of the cosmic balance itself. The artifacts, their power tempered by the hands of the chosen ones, served as a reminder of the triumph of unity and hope over the cosmic mysteries.

Emberwood, once a town besieged by shadows and cosmic threats, was now a town basking in the radiant light of victory. And as the sun set in the distance, its warm rays illuminating the town's rejuvenated beauty, Elara knew that their story was far from over.

The echoes of destiny and the prophecies that had guided them were but threads in the vast tapestry of the universe. Emberwood, with its enduring spirit, stood as a beacon of hope—a testament to the power of unity, courage, and the unwavering belief that even in the face of the cosmic mysteries, the human heart could shine bright, illuminating the path to a future where hope would always prevail.

And so, beneath the vast expanse of the night sky, Elara and the people of Emberwood embraced the infinite possibilities of the cosmos. The echoes of destiny, once enigmatic and daunting, were now a source of inspiration and wonder. The town, once plagued by shadows and ancient prophecies, was now a sanctuary of strength and courage.

Emberwood, with its indomitable spirit, stood as a testament to the resilience of the human heart. And as the stars twinkled overhead, their light illuminating the town's rejuvenated beauty, Elara faced the future with a sense of awe, her heart alight with the promise of a universe where unity and courage would always triumph over the cosmic uncertainties.

And so, in the heart of Emberwood, the echoes of destiny became a melody—a harmonious symphony that echoed through the cosmos. The town, once threatened by shadows and ancient prophecies, now stood as a guardian of the cosmic balance itself. The artifacts, their power tempered by the hands of the chosen ones, served as a reminder of the triumph of unity and hope over the cosmic mysteries.

Emberwood, once a town besieged by shadows and cosmic threats, was now a town basking in the radiant light of victory. And as the sun set in the distance, its warm rays illuminating the town's rejuvenated beauty, Elara knew that their story was far from over.

The echoes of destiny and the prophecies that had guided them were but threads in the vast tapestry of the universe. Emberwood, with its enduring spirit, stood as a beacon of hope—a testament to the power of unity, courage, and the unwavering belief that even in the face of the cosmic mysteries, the human heart could shine bright, illuminating the path to a future where hope would always prevail.

And so, beneath the vast expanse of the night sky, Elara and the people of Emberwood embraced the infinite possibilities of the cosmos. The echoes of destiny, once enigmatic and daunting, were now a source of inspiration and wonder. The town, once plagued by shadows and ancient prophecies, was now a sanctuary of strength and courage.

Emberwood, with its indomitable spirit, stood as a testament to the resilience of the human heart. And as the stars twinkled overhead, their light illuminating the town's rejuvenated beauty, Elara faced the future with a sense of awe, her heart alight with the promise of a universe where unity and courage would always triumph over the cosmic uncertainties.

And so, in the heart of Emberwood, the echoes of destiny became a melody—a harmonious symphony that echoed through the cosmos. The town, once threatened by shadows and ancient prophecies, now stood as a guardian of the cosmic balance itself. The artifacts, their power tempered by the hands of the chosen ones, served as a reminder of the triumph of unity and hope over the cosmic mysteries.

Emberwood, once a town besieged by shadows and cosmic threats, was now a town basking in the radiant light of victory. And as the sun set in the distance, its warm rays illuminating the town's rejuvenated beauty, Elara knew that their story was far from over.

The echoes of destiny and the prophecies that had guided them were but threads in the vast tapestry of the universe. Emberwood, with its enduring spirit, stood as a beacon of hope—a testament to the power of unity, courage, and the unwavering belief that even in the face of

the cosmic mysteries, the human heart could shine bright, illuminating the path to a future where hope would always prevail.

And so, beneath the vast expanse of the night sky, Elara and the people of Emberwood embraced the infinite possibilities of the cosmos. The echoes of destiny, once enigmatic